TABLE OF CONTENTS

DEDICATION

To my family with my love. Their ever present love means everything.

©Marion Pond 1982
Library of Congress #82-71114
ISBN 0-941284-13-1

Printed by *United Litho*, Falls Church, VA
Color Separations by *Falcon Color*, Washington, DC
Typesetting by *Type Too Ltd*, Rockville, MD
Color Photography by *Dan Glass*, Reston, VA
B&W Photography by *Allison Studio*, Newburyport, MA

Front cover features *"Wildflowers and Bee"* design by
Sherry Nelson, and cut and pierce, and easy watercolor
method by the author.

CONTINUING THE TRADITION

Shades of Yesteryear is an introduction to the lovely old art of making and decorating lampshades. While many of the popular decorative art forms will be presented, special emphasis is placed on the technique of cutting and piercing. (Cutting and piercing involves slitting, and punching holes into the shade paper to create a design. Curving the cut sections, and sometimes adding colored tints or colored lining papers further enhance the appearance.) A frosted acetate cover is added to protect and help preserve the lovely work. While the acetate wrap is not necessary, it is desirable and adds a fine finishing touch.

After the basics of lampshade making are learned, you can extend this craft as far as your imagination and experimentation will take you. The lighting in your home can then be much more than a mere source of light. It can, and should be an intricate part of your decorating theme as well as a lovely display of your artistic talent.

This book includes some basic instructions for application of cherished traditional art forms (stenciling, theorem, glass painting, watercolors, folk art, and trapunto) onto lampshade materials. Each category, however, is an art in itself, so in-depth instructions of each cannot be properly covered in one book. References for additional information and instructions are listed in the back of this book.

It is my sincere hope you will not only learn to make well constructed lampshades, but will enjoy using the decorative arts to enhance them.

My motto is:

"Whatever you do, do it on a lampshade!"

Why learn to make a lampshade? Have you ever shopped for a new shade and traveled miles looking? If you are lucky you might find just the right one, but you most likely won't like the price. The "something special" feeling of making your own lampshade, which can be displayed for years with pride and enjoyment, makes it worth doing.

SUPPLIES

MATERIALS

This is the way it all begins. From flat papers, round rings, glue and ribbons, we'll set out to construct a sturdy, beautiful lampshade. You can obtain these materials at hobby and craft shops. Additionally, a source listing is provided at the back of the book.

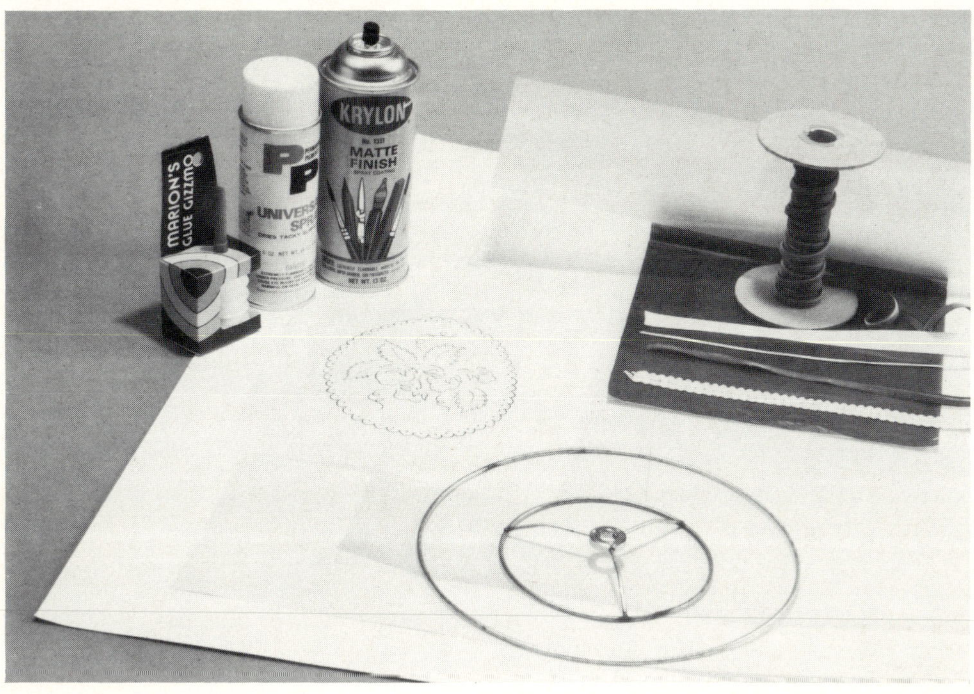

Rings (To make a small shade you will need two rings, 10" in diameter for the bottom and 6" in diameter for the top)

Pattern (The pattern shown on pages 24 and 25 fits the above rings)

Design (Several designs are provided in this book)

Shade paper (A sturdy paper; is the main component of the shade)

Lining paper (A thin, translucent paper; adds a special touch to the cut and pierced shade when lighted)

Frosted Acetate (Used as a protective cover; serves as surface for "glass painting" techniques)

Tracing paper (Thin transparent paper; used to copy designs)

Transfer paper (Graphite - used for transferring your tracing to the shade paper)

Matte spray (Provides a protective finish to shade papers)

Grosgrain ribbon (Binds edges of the shade)

Braid and Velvet (Add the decorative, finishing touch)

Not pictured: **brads** (for fastening seams of acetate wrap), **polyester fiber** (for use with the Trapunto technique), **pressure sensitive adhesive backing** (for strengthening fabrics and thin papers)

TOOLS

Assemble the following items for use in working with the lampshade papers and materials:

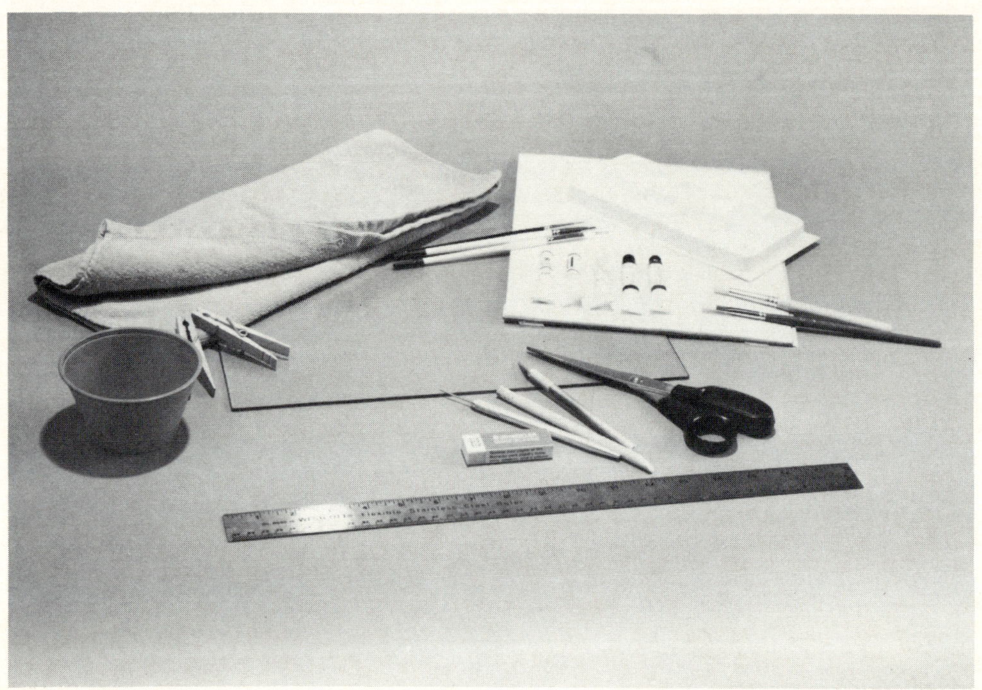

Glass (approx. 10" x 14", extra thick -provides the smooth surface upon which the design is cut)

Scissors

Cutting knife (hobby or craft knife)

Piercers (two, a large and small; or needles stuck into pieces of cork)

Towel (acts as a cushion under shade paper during piercing)

Eraser (Mars or kneaded)

Sharp pencil

Paints (oils and watercolors)

Palette

Damp rag

Wooden spring type clothespins (as shown on page 28)

Ruler

Glue Gizzmo (or heavy white glue)

Brushes (Loew Cornell)
Flats, Series 7300 - #4, #6, #8 (or substitute Series 797-F)
Rounds, Series 7350 - #0, #1
Stencil, Series 1136 - #3 (small)
Theorem, Series 1025 - #4

Not pictured; wax paper, toothpicks, paper towels

GENERAL INFORMATION

LAMPSHADE PAPERS

My search for papers which could be used for lampshade making has been quite an education. I am sure there is still much to learn in this area, and I look forward to continued development of other beautiful papers and materials. The discovery of new papers has been a great part of the fun as I have progressed with lampshade making.

The paper must be strong enough not to collapse when working with it, and not so heavy that it will be difficult to cut. The paper should be transparent enough to allow the light and color to shine through. If the paper is too dense, the light will only reflect out the top and bottom of the shade. When unlit, the shade itself just becomes a dark shape. When lit, different papers of varying textures add interest to an otherwise plain shade. You will find this aspect of selecting papers ever so interesting, and soon you will come to appreciate papers that also enhance the shade when illuminated.

Colored papers are pretty, but, here again, how they look when light is passing through is important. I prefer duplex papers for lampshade making because the white paper on the inside reflects twice as much light as a paper that is dark on both sides. Some duplex papers look like woven fabric when illuminated, which is an extra bonus.

PATTERNS

A pattern is the outline that will determine the size and shape of your lampshade. Once a pattern is transferred to your shade paper, it is referred to as the *arc*.

There are three ways to obtain a pattern:

1. You can purchase patterns from your lampshade materials supplier.
2. You may draft your own. It is too lengthy a project to cover in this book. If you should care to learn how, the information is given in detail in Ruth Dorsman's book, *Sculptured Lampshades.*
3. Use an old shade to make a pattern. To do so, remove the trim and binding, being careful not to destroy the shade paper. Open the back seam. A craft knife makes this job easier. Remove the rings. The old shade paper is now your pattern to use for making a new shade.

A pattern for a small shade is included in this book on pages 24 and 25. Trace the pattern and double it for the complete arc pattern.

GLUE

I cannot stress enough the importance of being very careful when applying glue. It can be the difference between a professional looking lampshade and a "hodgepodge." I have seen handmade shades in shops that were ruined by a messy glue job. Use of the proper glue (thick, quick drying, clear, suitable for paper and fabrics) can make your job easy. Some glues are too wet and runny, or too slow drying, or may not stick well to all the different materials required in making a lampshade. If you have ever struggled with the wrong glue, or tried to make a fine line with a brush or toothpick, you will appreciate the **Glue Gizzmo,** (shown on pages 22 and 23). It solves all of these problems and will help you attain a neat finished shade.

RINGS

Rings provide the stabilizing support for the papers. Rings which are nickel plated and lacquer dipped are desirable as they will not rust. Some rings are heavier weight than others. Test your rings to your pattern by clothespinning the pattern on the rings. If you do not have an overlapping seam of about ½" you should add to the pattern by drawing the needed amount on one seam edge.

The most common rings used are:

> Clip top ring
> Bottom ring
> Washer top ring
> Uno top ring

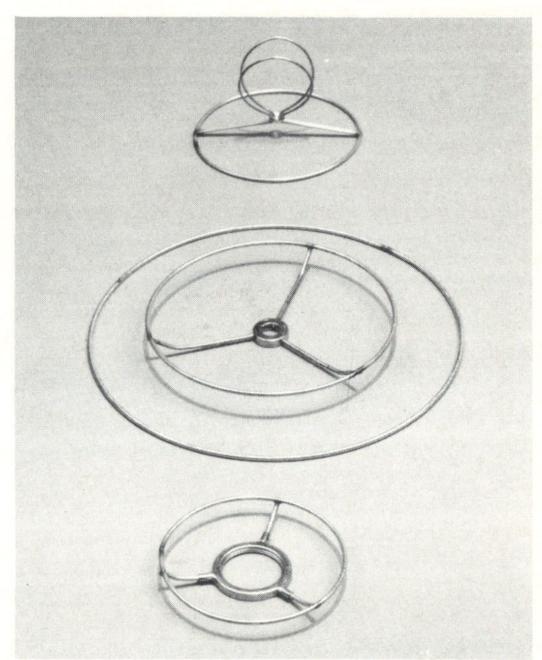

FROSTED ACETATE

Have you ever come home with a new shade and been tempted to leave that unattractive protective cover on? I have, with the thought of keeping it clean and extending its life. That is the Yankee in me, and that is no doubt why I favor an acetate cover or wrap.

Acetate wrap is an option. However, it is very desirable on white or light colored papers and especially on cut and pierced lampshades. Once you spend time and money to make a lovely shade, protect it. The acetate I use is 10 mil. thick (.010). Acetate is not made with lampshade making in mind, so we must contend with slight imperfections. (Most imperfections will usually not show when the shade is assembled.)

Acetate is very magnetic and will pick up dust and eraser crumbs. And, it just loves cat and dog hair (of which I currently have too many). Helpful hint: If you end up with "stuff" on the acetate, lightly spray a lint free rag with static guard and wipe the shiny side just before adding it to the shade. The acetate can be cleaned with window cleaner.

TRIMS

Trimming is fun for it provides the opportunity to use a wide variety of colors. I almost think a living could be made just retrimming store shades. AH - food for thought!!

In this book, I have used grosgrain ribbon (pronounced grow-grain), braid, velvet and soutache.

Grosgrain is more an integral part of the construction than a decoration. It should be about 50/50 cotton and rayon. Most grosgrains on the market are polyesters (great for sewing, but not for lampshades). Polyester does not glue well or stretch well, and we need a ribbon that will do both. Size #5 is used.

Braid is pretty and easy to work with. It is often best for your first lampshade. It will cover many imperfections in the application of the grosgrain.

Velvet is my favorite trim. The shades of color available make it easy to add just the right touch of color for the perfect finishing accent. Use a good quality velvet that is crush and shine proof, and is about 50/50 nylon and rayon. Size #1½ is used.

Soutache is a thin cord which I like to use to pick up just a little additional color when using velvet trim.

PRESSURE SENSITIVE MATERIAL (ADHESIVE BACKED)

There are two types of pressure sensitive materials that I use in lampshade making: paper and plastic. These are used as backing for materials which are flimsy. To determine which pressure sensitive material to use, keep these factors in mind. *Pressure sensitive paper* is dense and will not allow much light through it. It is used for thin fabric or papers which would lose detail and color when illuminated. *Pressure sensitive plastic* (styrene or vinyl) is semi-transparent and is used with heavy fabric to allow more light to shine through.

FASTENERS

Brads (brass fasteners) are used on a lampshade seam when the shade is covered with frosted acetate. Since acetate is transparent, a glued seam would show through and be most unattractive. Brads hold neatly, and if painted the color of the shade paper, they are much more attractive than a glued seam. Glue may be used, however, to fasten the seam on all other materials.

SPRAY

A clear matte spray can be used to protect the shade paper and its painting. I suggest you first test the spray on a scrap of paper for discoloration, spotting, or too much shine. The spray is not to be used on the acetate.

SELECTING THE SHADE

DETERMINING THE RIGHT SIZE. There are no firm rules for this, so you will see all sorts of extremes. However some safe guidelines are:

1. On a short, fat base, use a short, fat shade.
2. On a tall, slim base, use a tall, slim shade.
3. Make the height of the shade approximately the same as the height of the base, excluding the lighting fixtures.

COMPLEMENTING THE BASE. Again, there are no specific rules. If the base is plain, I take this opportunity to decorate the shade, and it then becomes the focal point. I feel the shade has been neglected as a decorating accessory for too long. If the base is the focal point, then do not detract from it with a busy shade. Complement it with plain papers or fabric trim to color coordinate it.

DESIGNS FOR CUT AND PIERCE LAMPSHADES

The designs on the following pages were made especially for cutting and piercing. You need not limit yourself to these, however. Designs seem to be everywhere you look. Simple designs, such as in coloring books, adapt very easily. Even complicated designs will work well if one omits all unnecessary details.

1. Make a tracing of any design which pleases you, being careful not to connect any lines to form an enclosed area. (See page 19). If lines are connected the section would fall out creating a hole when the lines were cut.

2. Widen the spacing between objects, if necessary. Lines too close, when cut, will weaken that area of the paper.

Here is an example of how any design may be converted into a cut and pierce design. Long lines are broken and spaces are inserted. No area should be totally enclosed, or, like the hole in a doughnut, it will drop out.

*Transfer design to **back** side of shade paper; cut and pierce from the **back**; mold and shape from the **back.***

A solid line is shown here for convenience in tracing.
Use it as a guide for piercing only. Do not cut along it.

Subtle color may be added by using a pastel lining paper under the white arc, creating a soft glow of color when the lamp is turned on.

Cut and pierced designs are very elegant and quite formal looking done in only white (white arc lined with white lining paper).

The cut and pierce technique can also be used on a colored paper.

Keep the bugs out! Bugs love light and will often go to extremes to get to it - even if it means crawling through strawberries, daisies, borders, and whatever else one might dream up to cut and pierce on a lampshade. Once trapped amidst the beautifully curving designs they may be destined to reside there forever.

You can save these little beasties from entrapment and preserve your beautiful handiwork by adding an acetate wrap. This one extra step is often omitted by shade makers. But when you care enough to make the best, why not care enough to protect it. Besides, the acetate wrap is to a cut and pierced shade what a hand rubbed finish is to fine furniture.

Lampshades have been sadly neglected in the home decorating scheme. Your family and friends will immediately recognize what a lovely addition a personalized lampshade makes.

Color page: Acrylic folk art borders and two cut and pierce designs.

INSTRUCTIONS FOR MAKING A CUT AND PIERCE LAMPSHADE

In this section, the following steps will be covered:

1. Cutting the arc
2. Cutting the acetate
3. Tracing and transferring the design
4. Piercing
5. Cutting
6. Molding and shaping the design
7. Lining and glueing
8. Constructing the shade
9. Wrapping with acetate
10. Trimming and adding braid

These instructions include the cutting and piercing of a strawberry design (design is on page 11), and the basic construction for any size lampshade using two rings. The lampshade we will be making is a 6" x 10" x 7½", a common and useful size.

CUTTING THE ARC

Before tracing the arc pattern onto the shade paper, be sure the table surface is clean, and hands are washed to remove any oil. Lay the pattern on the shade paper and draw around it with a pencil (no pens). Cut along the pencil lines. You now have the lampshade arc. Erase pencil lines from the straight seam edges. (The other edges do not matter as they will be trimmed away later.) Use a white eraser (Mars or kneaded). Do not use a pencil eraser as it will leave marks on the paper.

At this point, decide which side of the paper you want for the front side (some papers are more textured on one side than on the other). Once selected, make a small pencil mark at the very top edge so you will know the front side.

CUTTING THE ACETATE

Cut a matching piece of frosted acetate. Place the acetate on the table with the frosted side up. Lay the shade paper arc (front side up) on top of the acetate. Draw around the paper, transferring a pattern to the acetate. Cut the acetate, being careful to cut straight seam edges, removing the pencil lines (seams only) as you cut. Be careful to keep the acetate clean. After cutting it out, place it in a clean area as it will attract lint and dust.

Clean up your act! Clean hands and a clean work area help assure you of a nice, clean, finished product.

TRACING AND TRANSFERRING THE DESIGN

Copy the design to be cut and pierced onto tracing paper. (A tracing makes it possible to see through to the pattern for proper placement when transferring it to your shade paper.) Trace very carefully to avoid problems when it comes to cutting the design. *Important: Do not connect lines!* Unlike a stencil, you do not want to cut a piece out. Also, lines must not be too close together.

Transfer the design onto the back side of the shade by centering it horizontally. Vertically, it may be placed in the center or lower, but no closer than an inch and a half from the bottom edge. Use graphite paper (not carbon as it is greasy and makes a mess). Place graphite paper under the traced design and re-trace lines. Use a sharp pencil with light pressure. Transfer lightly, just enough design to be barely seen. Try not to have thick, dark lines. The piercing and cutting of the design will be done from the back side.

Figure 1

PIERCING

Since it is easier to pierce the design (poke holes to represent stems, tendrils, etc.) while the paper is intact, it is usually done before cutting. Place a folded towel under the design area of your shade to receive the needle (piercer) as you poke it through the paper. A design may or may not tell you where to pierce. In many instances, it is a matter of choice. Often the stems and the veins in leaves are pierced. I generally prefer to cut both of these, however, and to pierce borders and flower centers and curly cues or tendrils. My reason for this is that cut lines are bolder and easier to paint (should one decide to add color to the design). Experiment to see which you prefer. I most often use the small piercer on small flowers, and the larger piercer on big, bold flowers.

Punch the piercer through the paper, keeping the spacing even. Do not be unreasonably fussy. Be careful, however, not to have the punches too close as this will weaken the paper. Example ...

Piercing

CUTTING

Remove the towel and replace it with a piece of extra thick glass (about 10" x 14"). Now comes the work! Unless you are used to cutting with a sharp craft knife or stencil cutting knife, your fingers will get a little tired. Some of my designs are deliberately small so as not to "paralyze" your hand on your first try. Cut only until your hand tires, then rest for a while. Practice first on a piece of scrap.

Press hard enough to cut clean through on the first pass. To have to re-cut often causes rough edges. Check to make sure the cut is completely through and will open easily. On curves, such as petals, turn the paper, as you slowly pull the knife towards you. Your knife hand hardly changes position as you turn the paper with your free hand. Move the paper and see what nice smooth cuts this makes. (Now try keeping the paper in one place and move just the knife. The cuts will be choppy and require greater effort with less success.) Practice repeatedly and it will soon be smooth and easy.

Cutting on glass

Now that you have mastered curves, try leaves. Begin at the base of the leaf and cut towards the tip. Do not remove the knife but tilt it straight up on it's point and swing the paper until it is heading in the other direction. Then continue cutting. If you cut down to the point from both sides, you run the risk of crossing the cut. (See Figure 2).

If you slip and over-cut, do not panic. Put a piece of scotch tape over the spot, tap the spot with the back end of your knife. This will mash the paper spreading it and closing up the cut. (It will never show on the front, honest!)

MOLDING AND SHAPING

This is easy and such a relief after cutting. You still are working from the back side of the shade. Pick up just enough of a leaf or petal to get your fingers under it, then gently, and a little at a time, curve it. *Do not bend or crease the paper*. Instead, gradually mold it. Bends will show from the front, and can make a curved petal look cut off. Bent edges can also lay back down and not let much light shine through. Well molded leaves and petals will hold their shape and create the desired shadows. In some small places where fingers are just too big, use the slanted end of the small piercer or orange stick, holding your finger in back for support. Straight cuts, such as those on a branch, should be opened and rolled in towards that subject.

Gentle molding and shaping

Completed design — back side of paper

Before going further, take a minute to check everything. Make sure all design lines are cut, opened, and molded.

Avoid crossing the cut.

Figure 2.

LINING AND GLUEING

Lining your cut and pierced shade is very desirable. It softens the light showing through the cuts. A colored lining adds a pleasant glow to the light and the design. It also hides the lamp bulb and fixtures. Colored lining paper does not change the color of your shade but adds that little extra touch when the light is turned on.

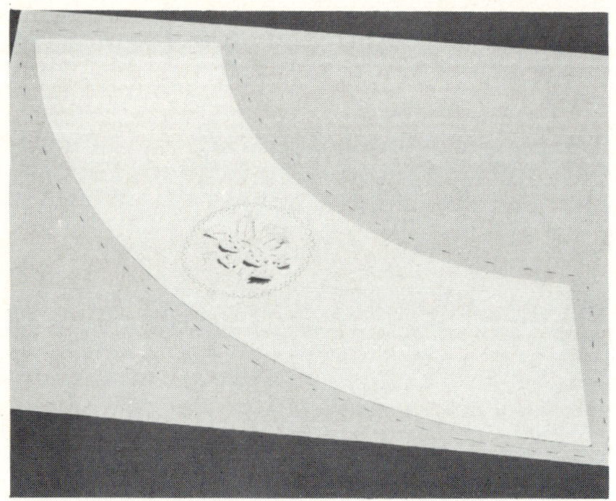

1. Place the lining paper on the table and lay your cut out shade on top. Mark a pencil line about ½" larger than the shade. Remove the shade paper and cut out the lining paper on the lines. Do not fuss, as the edges get trimmed later.

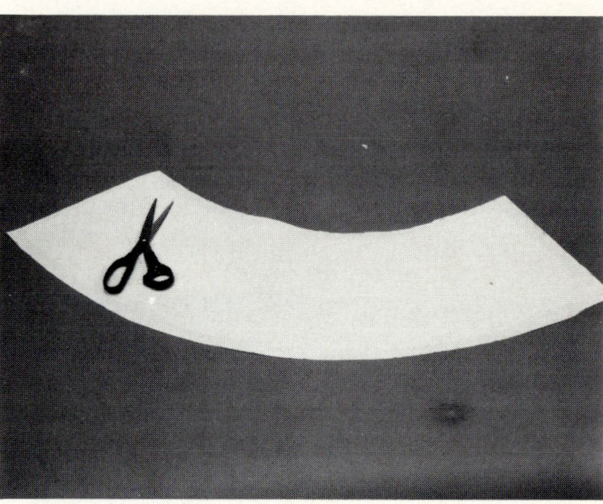

2. Now lay the lining paper right on top of the back of the shade paper. (The side you have been working so hard on). Place a weight (scissors will do) on the left side.

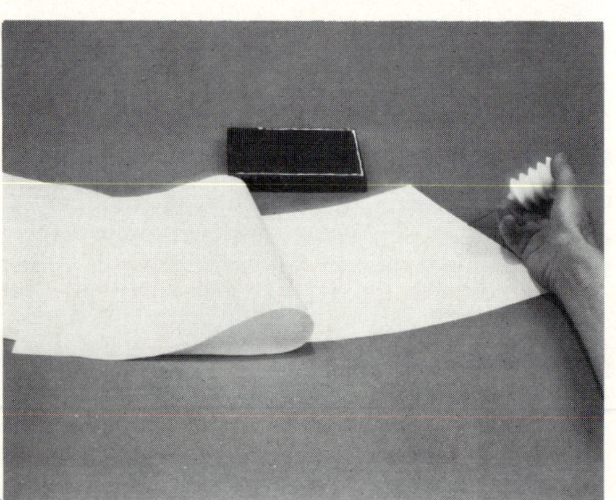

3. Turn about one third of the lining over to the left side. Starting at the right side, squeeze glue about eight inches along the top, down the seam, and then about eight inches along the bottom edge. (Glue should be in a very thin line close to the edge as illustrated on the black block.)

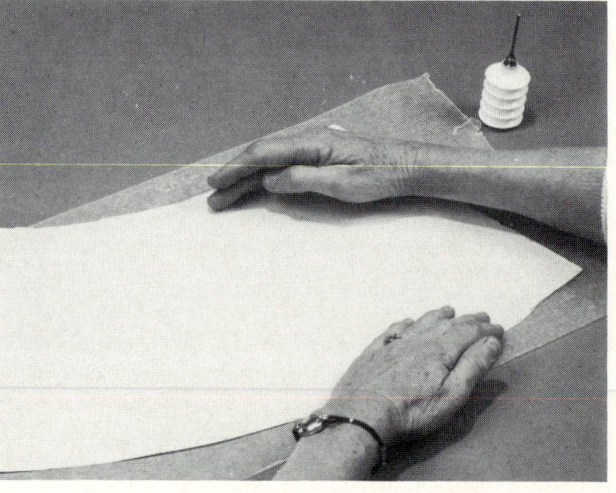

4. Lay lining paper back down on the glue and smooth out from top to bottom.

Note: You may want to protect your table from glue run-over by placing a piece of wax paper under your work.

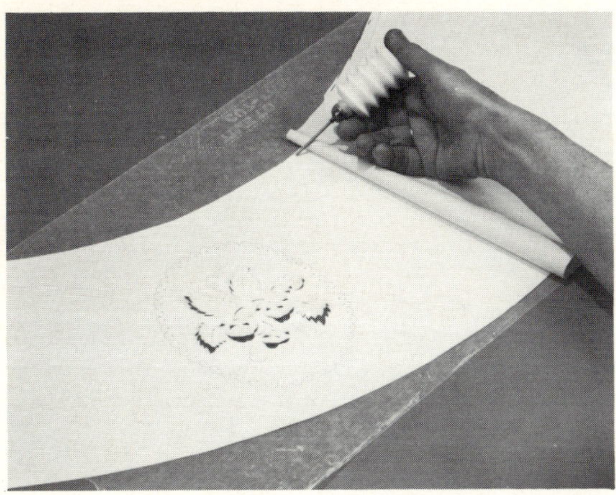

5. *Remove the weight and lift paper from the left. Lay it back to the glued section. Squeeze glue along the top and bottom. (Middle third of the shade).*

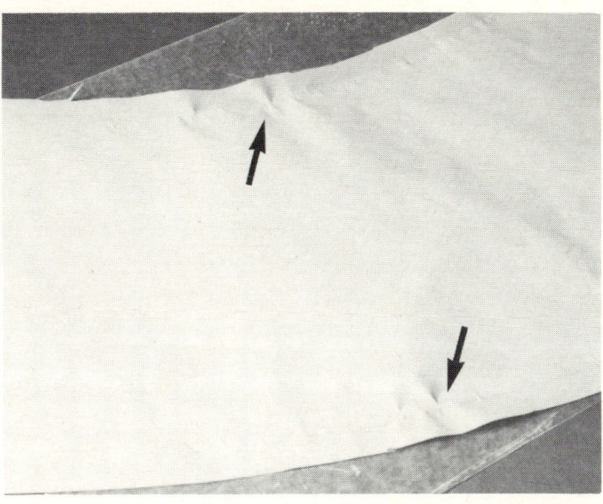

6. *Lay the lining paper back down, and smooth out from top to bottom. Avoid crushing your molded area. At this point, you may have to ease in a little fullness along the edges. Do not try to push fullness along to the end as it will accumulate. Instead, ease the fullness in gradually.*

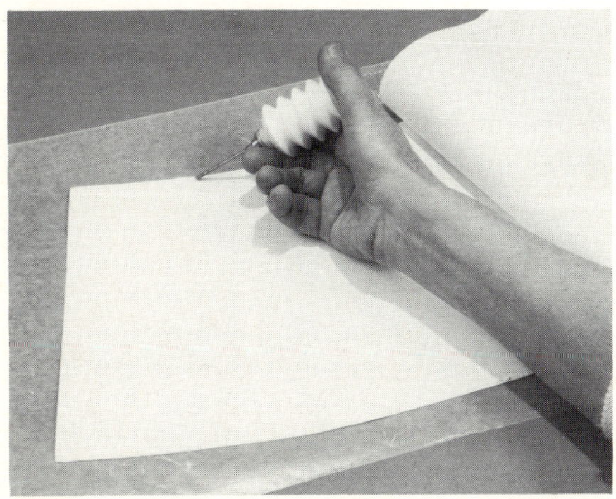

7. *Continue to glue the remaining section.*

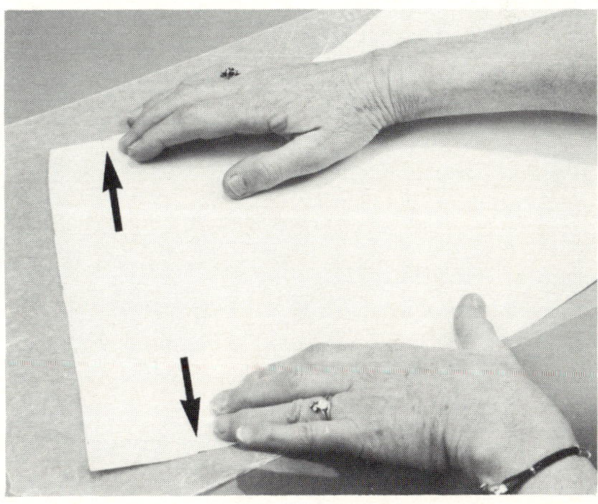

8. *Press lining paper out towards the edges.*

Cut and trim excess lining, being very careful to cut away all the lining paper from the straight seams. Seams can be cut neatly using a metal edge ruler and your cutting knife on the glass. The curved top and bottom edges can be cut with scissors or the knife. Do not be fussy along the edges because they are trimmed again after the rings are in place.

PATTERN

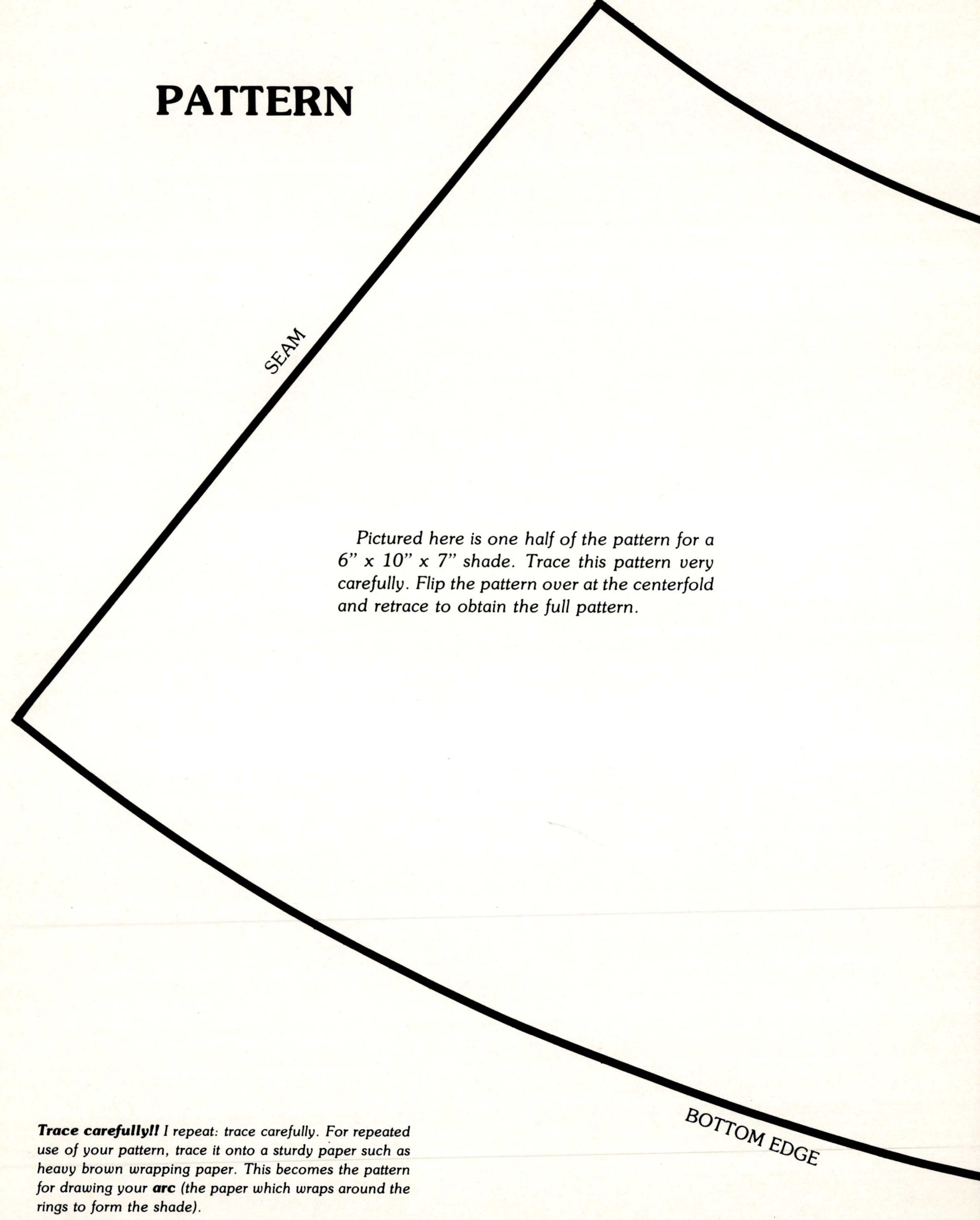

Pictured here is one half of the pattern for a 6" x 10" x 7" shade. Trace this pattern very carefully. Flip the pattern over at the centerfold and retrace to obtain the full pattern.

Trace carefully!! *I repeat: trace carefully. For repeated use of your pattern, trace it onto a sturdy paper such as heavy brown wrapping paper. This becomes the pattern for drawing your* **arc** *(the paper which wraps around the rings to form the shade).*

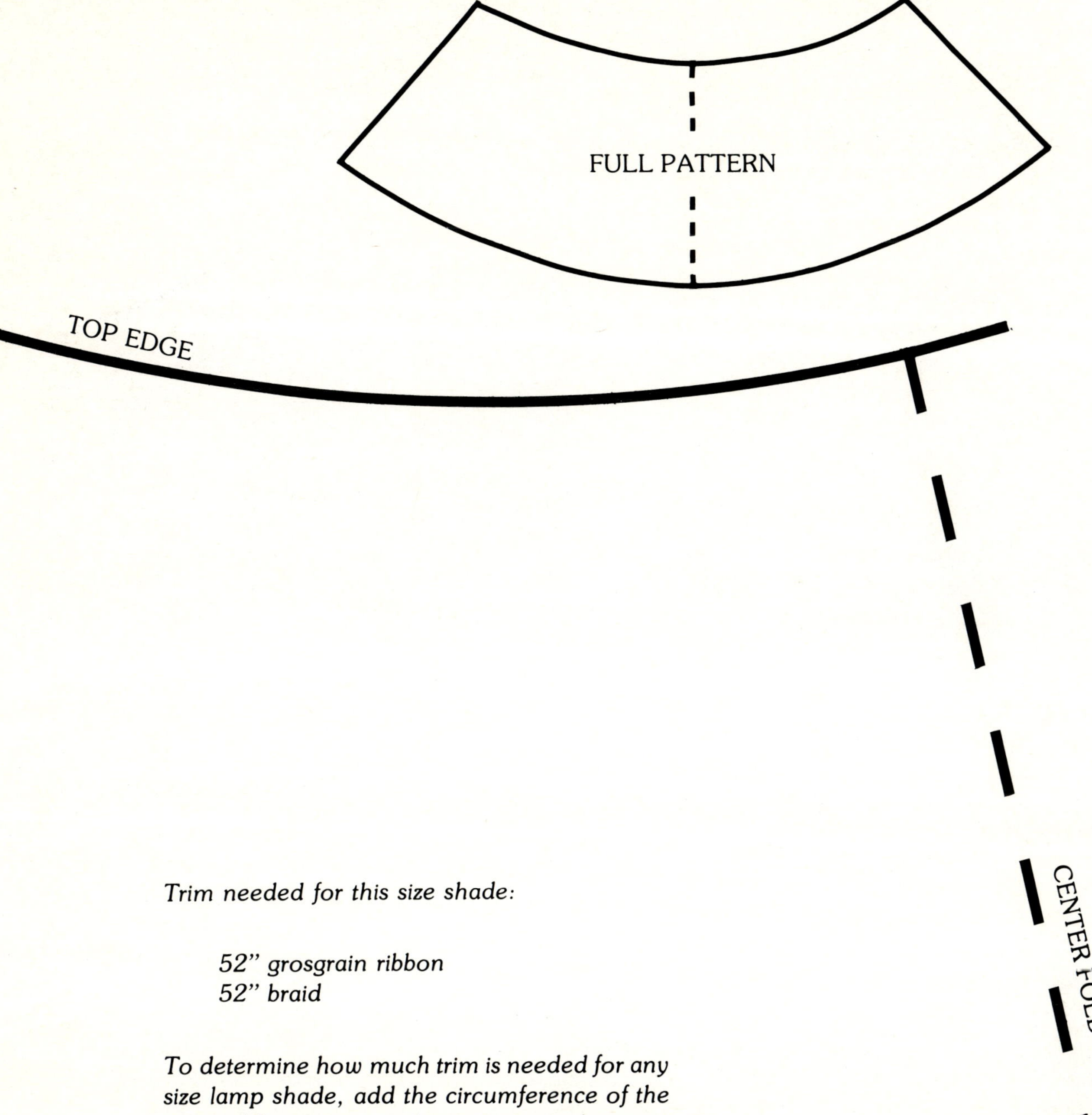

Trim needed for this size shade:

52" grosgrain ribbon
52" braid

To determine how much trim is needed for any size lamp shade, add the circumference of the top and bottom rings plus an extra inch or two for good measure!

CONSTRUCTION

Extra emphasis is placed on making a well constructed shade. It is a shame to see a lovely design or special painting spoiled by a poorly finished product.

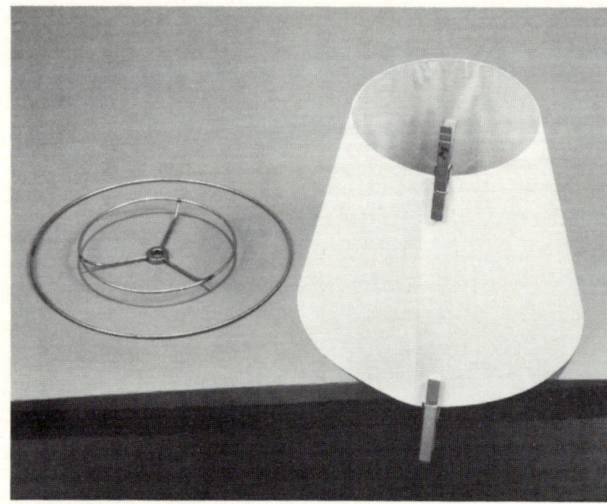

1. Wrap the shade to form into shape. Hold top and bottom together with wooden clothespins. Hang bottom pin over the table edge. Clothespins hold best if pushed down as far as they will go. When purchasing clothespins, look for ones with the spring recessed to allow you to push the clothespin down far enough to give a secure hold.

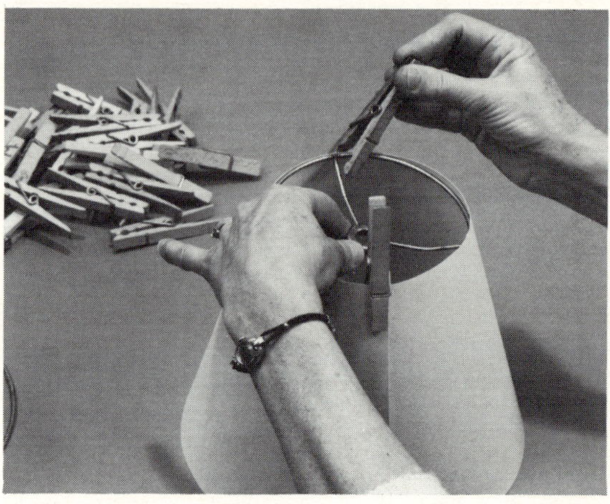

2. Place top ring under shade, spokes bending down. Reach down into the shade and pull the top ring up through, keeping a spoke in the front of the shade. Hold in place with a clothespin. (Seam is in the back, design is in the front). By placing a spoke in the front, it keeps the back seam area clear. This makes glueing or fastening the seam (a later step) easier to accomplish than if the spoke is in the way.

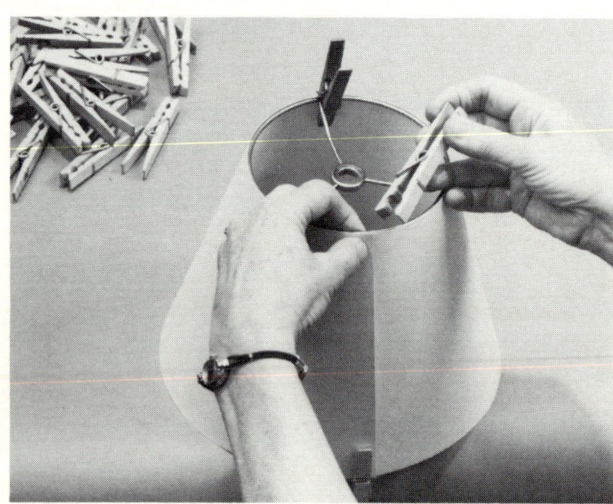

3. Remove the back clothespin. Position the ring to top and re-pin. Add about four more clothespins. Space them at random.

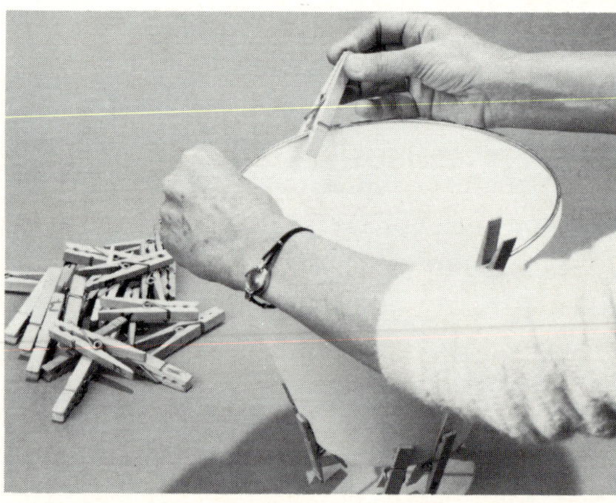

4. Flip the shade over and secure the bottom ring at the front edge with a clothespin.

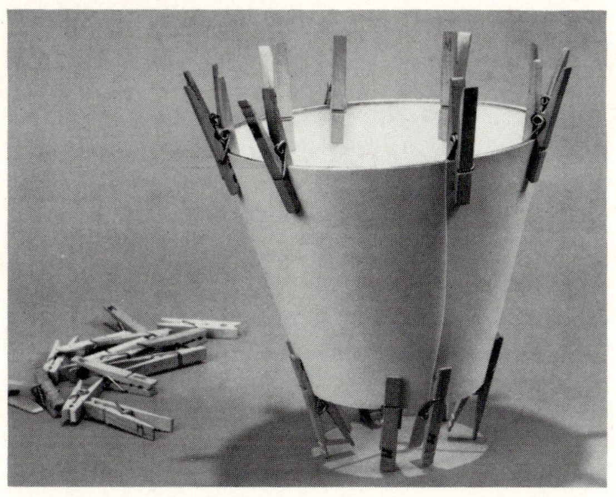

5. Ease the ring in and hold in position with about eight clothespins.

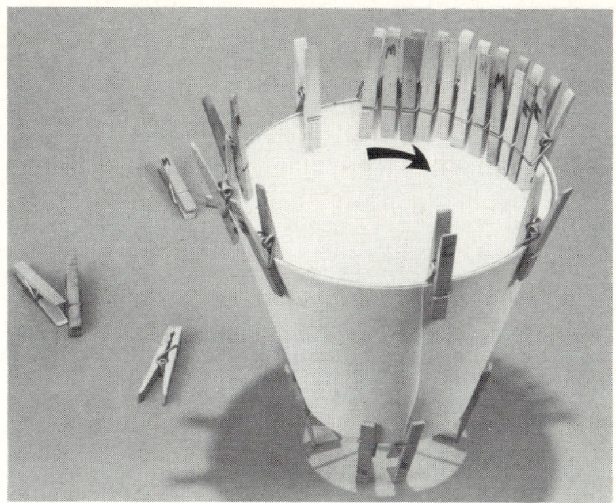

6. The paper must now be adjusted to fit snugly to the rings. The following method works well and saves problems later on. Position the shade, bottom up, with the seam facing you. Reach across the shade and start at the front center, placing one pin right after the other, moving clockwise. You will see any excess paper being moved along toward the seam by the "marching" pins. Go about half way to the seam, lift and replace remaining pins to let the excess move on and out. Add more pins as needed.

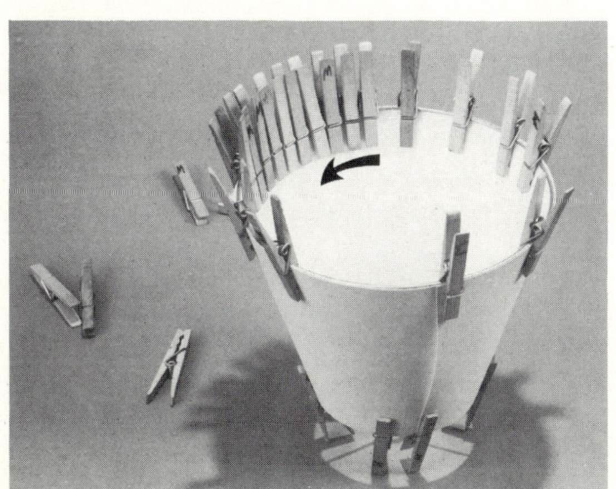

7. Now work from the center, moving counter clockwise. You may borrow some of the pins previously used to "march" on the left hand side. (I leave one pin and remove two, leave one and remove two, and so on.) Continue until you have moved all excess paper out to the seam. Turn your shade over and do the very same thing on the top ring.

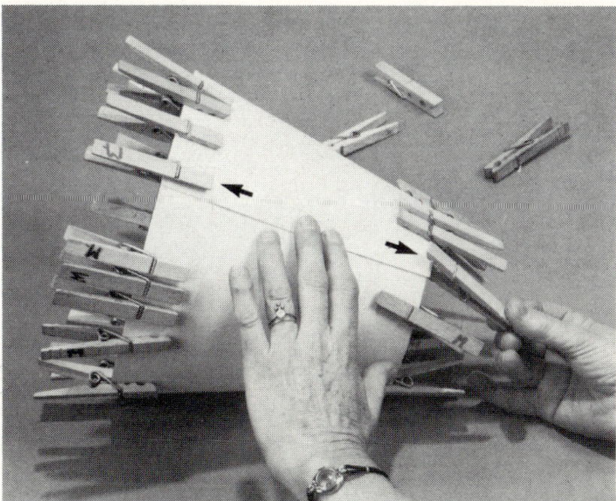

8. To lay the seam flat, remove the two pins holding it. Press center down flat and replace the pins.

If an acetate cover is not to be used, glue the seam. Then proceed with step 11.

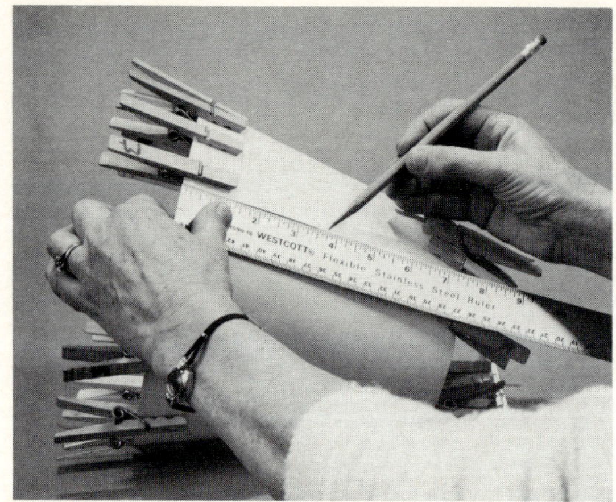

9. *Locate the center of the shade at the seam and mark a dot with a pencil. Measure 3/4" from the top and bottom rings, and mark the seam. This will locate three holes on the seam for brads.*

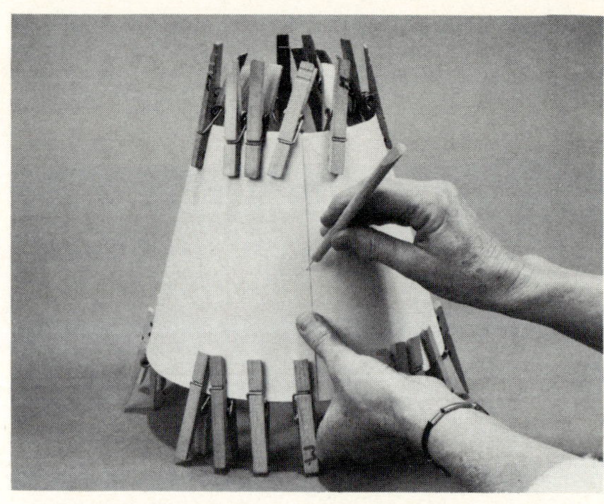

10. *Pierce the center hole, first with a small piercer, then with a larger one. Insert brad and open on the inside. Do the two remaining holes the same way.*

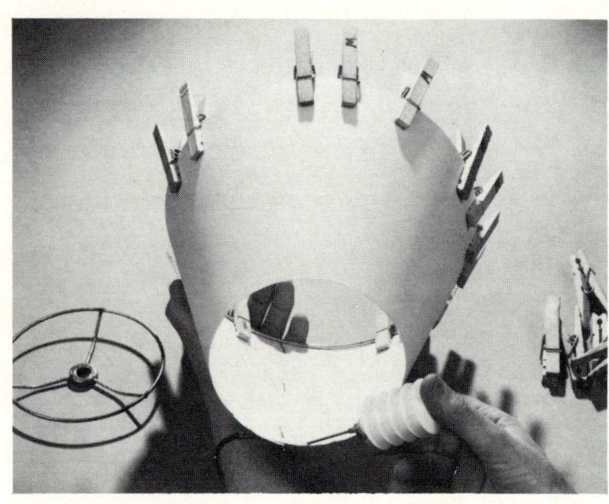

11. *Now that the paper fits tightly and the brads are in, you may remove the top ring and put a fine line of glue along the inside edge of the shade. Do not put too much, as you do not want glue extending down below the ring when it is put back in place. After the glue is applied, place the top ring on the table with spoke wires facing down. Place the shade on top of the ring and reach down inside pulling the ring up to the very top of your paper. Clothespin to hold. Your paper should fit tightly, so secure it with nine or ten clothespins.*

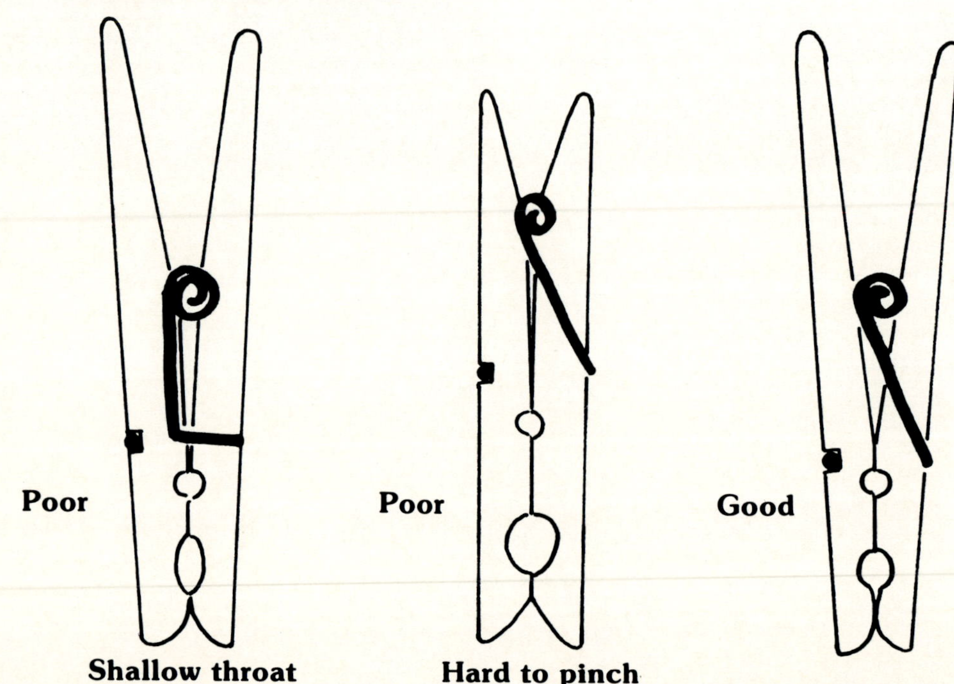

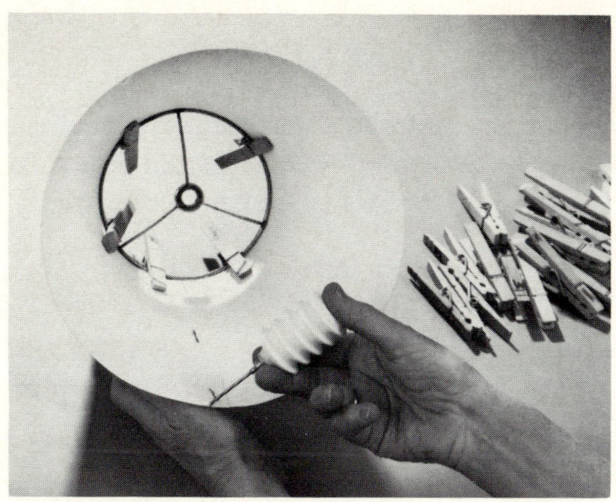

12. *Remove bottom ring and place a neat line of glue along the very bottom edge.*

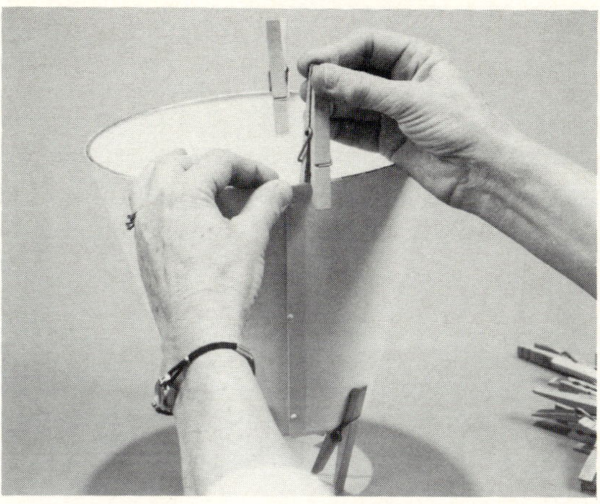

13. *Aim the ring into the front edge and secure with a clothespin. Ease the rest of the ring in and secure at back seam with a clothespin.*

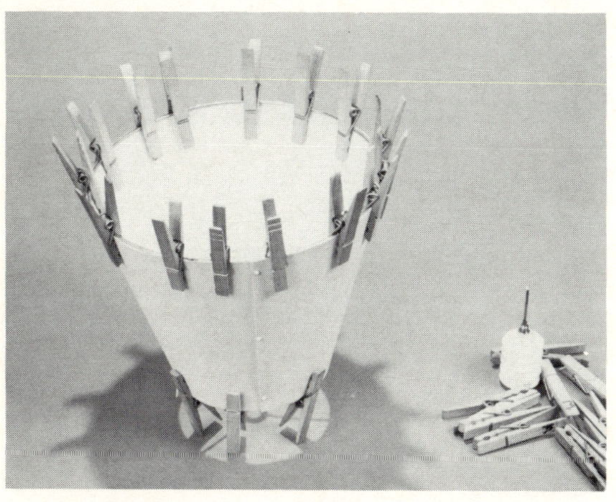

14. *Secure the ring with ten or twelve clothespin. Be sure both rings are flush to the edge of the paper. Let the glue set for about ten minutes. (This is a great time for a coffee break!)*

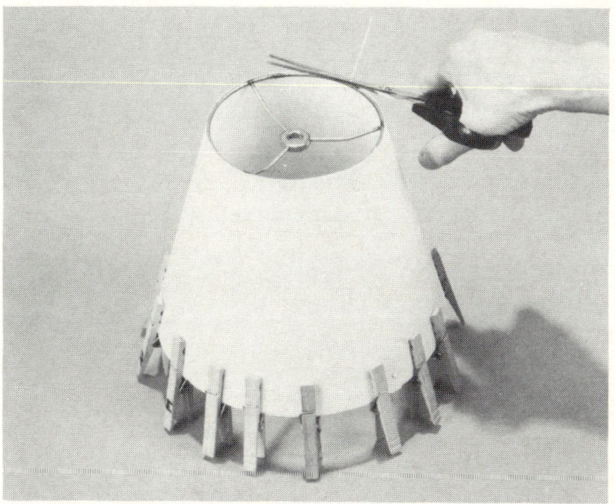

15. *Once the glue has set, remove the pins and scissor trim any paper which extends above the top of the ring. Angle the scissors and bear down so you will trim low, not just even. Repeat on the bottom ring. Now you are ready to add the acetate wrap.*

ACETATE WRAP

At this point, check for dirt or any foreign matter on your shade. The Mars eraser does wonders on the paper, but do not use it on the acetate. It will remove the frost and leave a shiny mark. If necessary, use window cleaner. Check the acetate for any specks, hair, etc., and remove them as described on page 6.

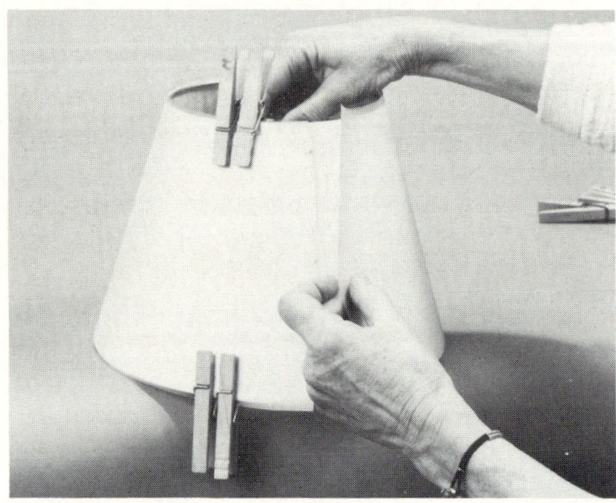

1. Wrap the acetate around the shade, lining up the seam edge of the shade with the seam edge of the acetate. Place two clothespins on top and two on the bottom about 1½" to 2" away from the seam. (The pins on the bottom edge need to hang over the edge of the table.)

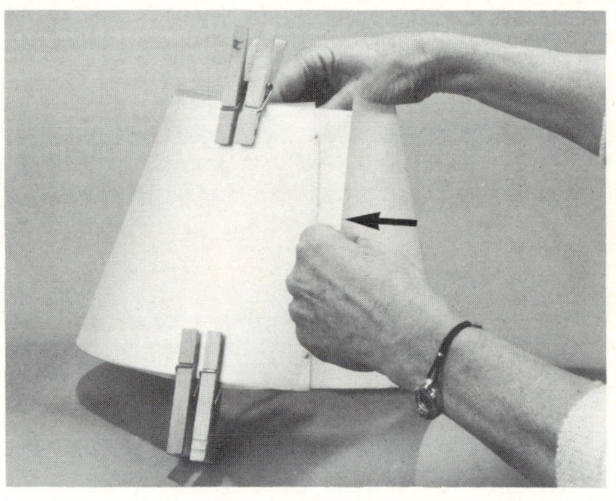

2. Pull the acetate snugly around the shade.

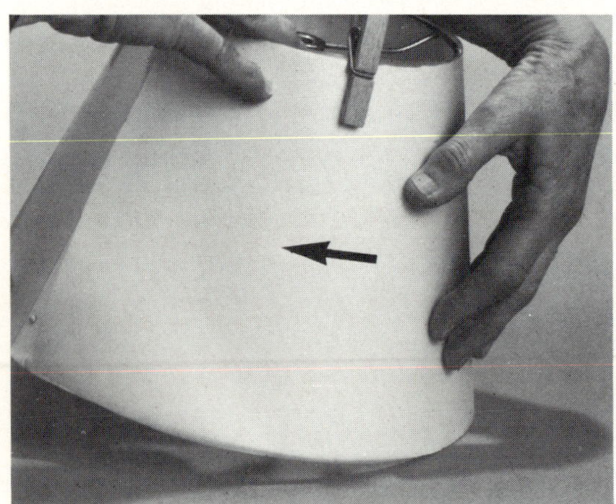

3. Place another clothespin on the top to hold the acetate, then work the acetate along towards the seam by pushing all loose material in the direction of the seam. (You will wish you had three or four hands.)

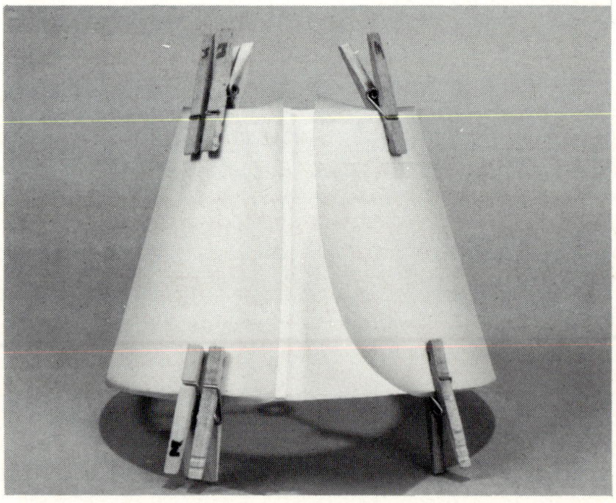

4. As you push the acetate and get it snug, secure it with clothespins.

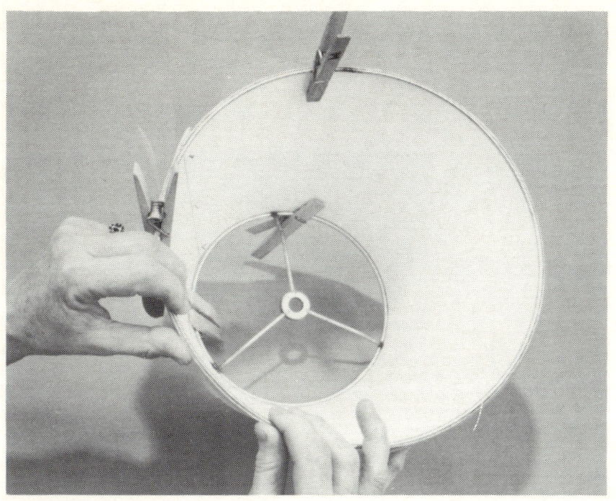

5. To tighten the acetate to the shade, lay the shade down and start at the first two clothespins (bottom of the shade) and push the acetate along for a few inches. Clothespin to hold. Then do the top, moving along a few inches at a time. This will work out any "slack". Continue this process, doing first the top, then the bottom, working all the way around. Do not worry if the acetate rides up a little on one edge as the excess will be trimmed away.

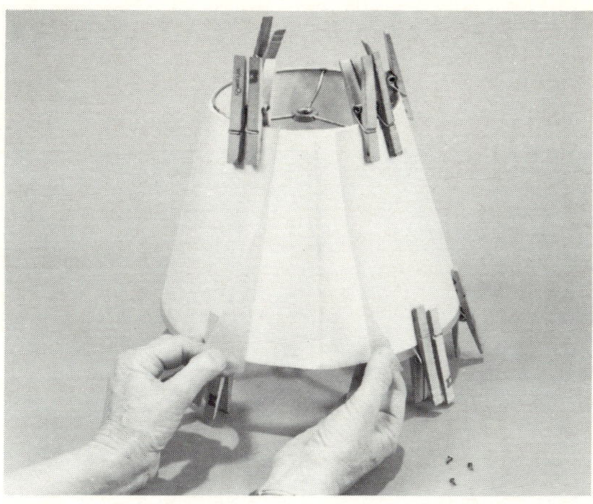

6. Place two clothespins about two inches back from each side of the seam on both the top and the bottom of the shade. Now remove the brads holding the lining and shade paper.

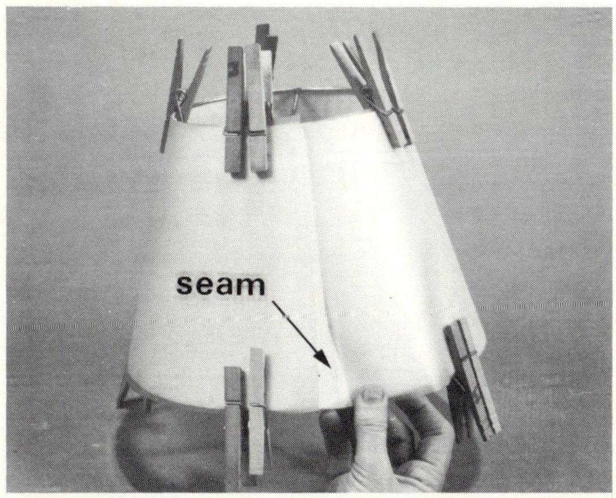

7. Slip one edge of the acetate into the shade paper seam.

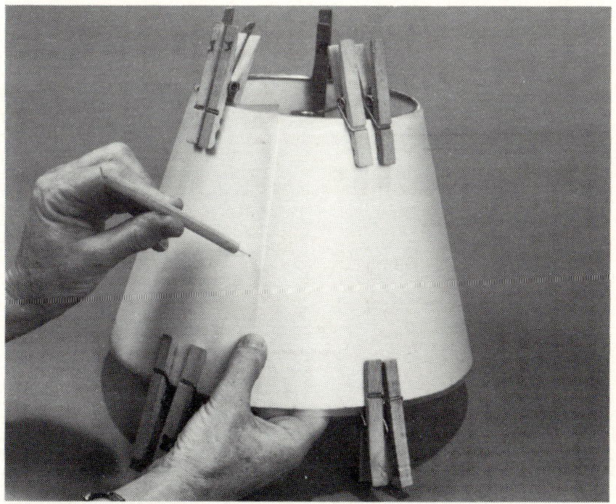

8. Place the other edge of the acetate over the seam and re-punch the holes, first with the small piercer, and then with the larger one. Replace the brads.

The acetate should now be in place and secure. Trim any acetate that extends above the top of the rings, as you did with the paper.

Note: Don't skimp and use inexpensive, thin acetate. It tends to expand with the heat of the light bulb and become permanently puckered. Settle for nothing less than 10 mil.

TRIMMING AND ADDING THE BRAID

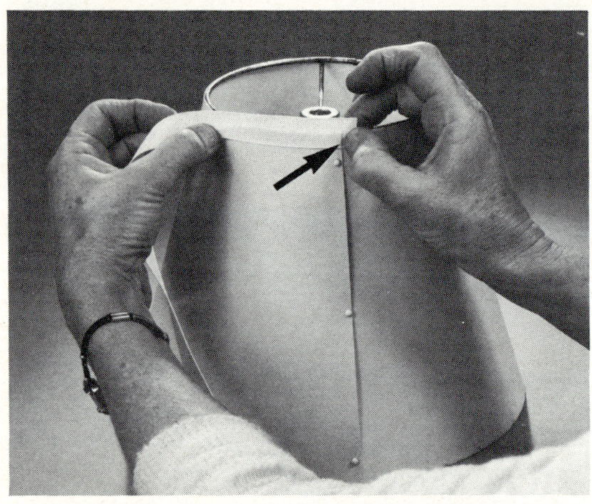

1. Apply glue on a few inches of grosgrain. Place the grosgrain on the shade with about half of it on the shade and half extending above. Stretch the bottom edge of the grosgrain as you apply it. This helps to get it nice and even. Push your thumbnail in at the seam to dent the grosgrain, as we will finish by butting the other end into this groove.

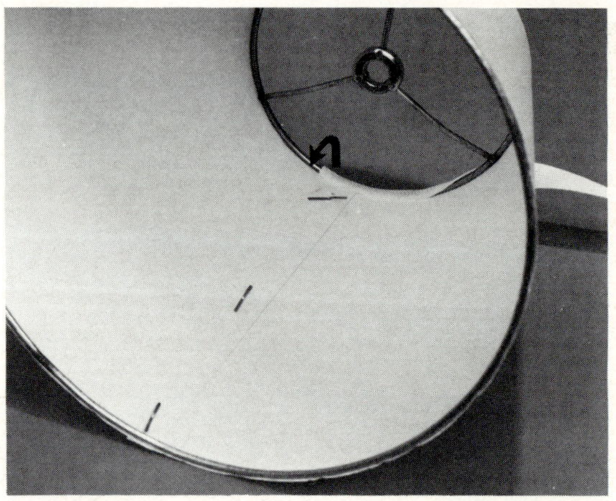

2. Roll the ribbon over the top and to the inside to wrap it around the ring. It should just cover the ring. Use your fingernail to push it in tight to the ring. It should not roll back onto the paper.

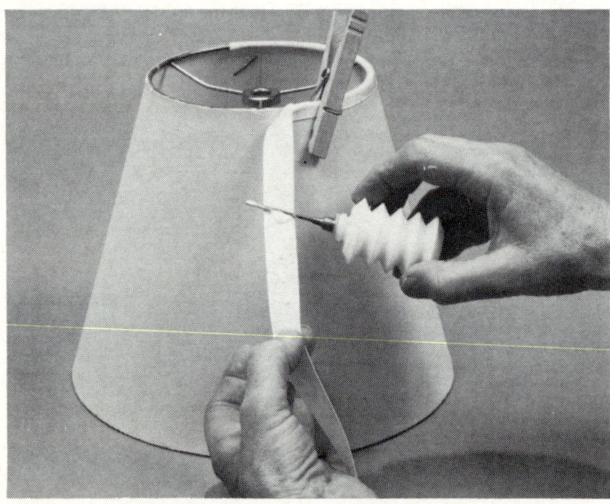

3. Place a clothespin on a slant to hold the grosgrain in place. Apply a few more inches of glue and spread it, being careful that the glue covers the very edge of the ribbon that wraps around the ring. Sufficient glue here is critical. the other edge does not matter as much. In fact, a sparse amount assures it will not "ooze" out onto the shade. If glue should get onto the shade, immediately wipe it with a damp paper towel.

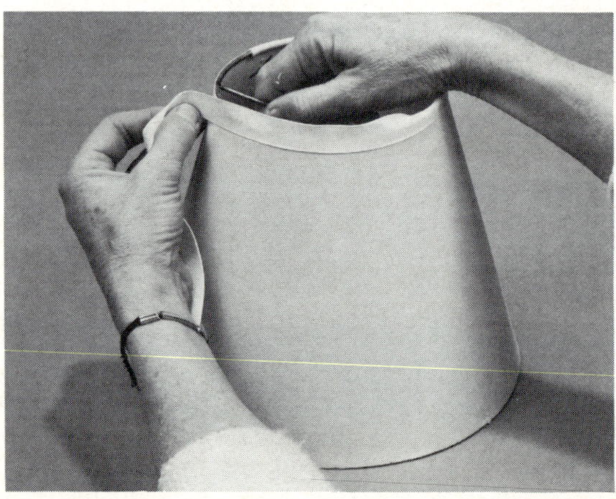

4. Stretch bottom edge, roll over and wrap and tuck in all the way around. Clip a notch out when you come to a spoke in the ring, then continue.

Color page: Wheat stencil and two trapunto designs.

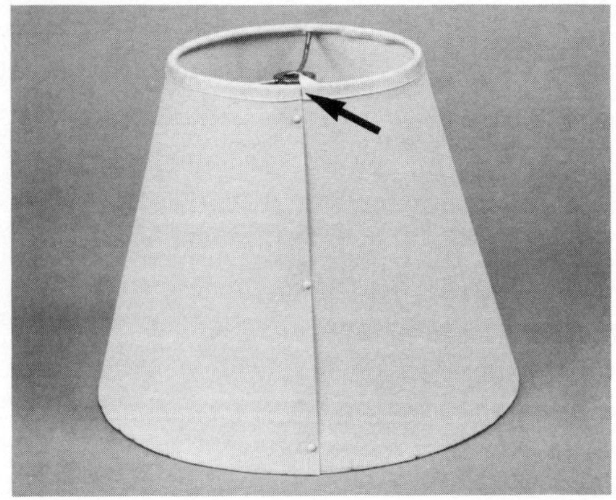

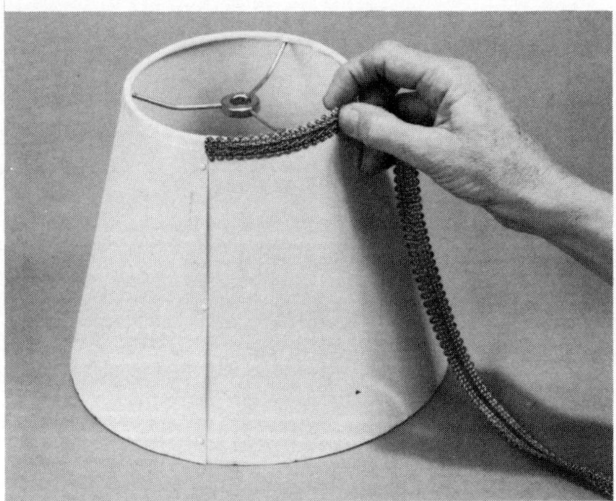

5. Cut off even at that dent you made earlier at the seam. Glue right into this groove. This makes a flat overlap.

*6. Place a little glue on the ends of the braid to keep them from raveling. Place glue on a few inches, just below the center of the braid. This is just trim. It is not holding anything together, so you need not extend glue out to the edges. The less glue, the better. Stretch as you go to keep it straight. If it is not straight, lift and replace. When you have worked around to the seam, cut even. You do not want to overlap the braid. Dab a little glue at the end and butt the braid right up to the beginning edge of braid. Add braid to the bottom in the same manner as you did the top. **Note:** Velvet ribbon may be substituted for the braid.*

Repeat the entire process to glue grosgrain to the bottom ring.

ADMIRE YOUR HANDIWORK

Stand back and admire your finished shade.

To appreciate the full impact of your decorative venture, place your shade on a lamp base containing a 60 watt bulb and turn on the light!

Caution: Use of larger than 40 watt bulbs with acetate thinner than 10 mil. may cause warping.

OTHER INTERESTING DECORATIVE TECHNIQUES

In addition to the cut and pierced technique, you might enjoy trying some of the other decorative art methods shown on the full color pages. These include:

Stenciling and Theorem painting on paper
Glass painting techniques - oil paints on acetate
Decorative folk art
Easy water color method for cut and pierced designs
Trapunto - sculpted fabric with adhesive backing material

Each of these methods is presented here merely as an introduction to the numerous decorative possibilities available to you for use in conjunction with lampshades.

STENCILING

Stenciling was used by early (and often traveling) craftsmen, especially in the East, to decorate walls and floors. Stenciling today retains the simplicity of these early craftsmen.

Trace the design onto stencil paper or Mylar. Paper is less expensive but is not as durable as Mylar. A stencil cut from Mylar will last indefinitely.

After tracing, follow instructions on "Cutting" in the Cut and Pierce section (page 20) except that each section is completely cut out. The paint is applied in this cut-out section. See directions below on applying paints.

APPLYING PAINT THROUGH STENCILS

Oils may be used successfully on paper if only a small amount of paint is applied. **Warning: too much paint will make an oily ring.** Oils have the transparency that is desirable on a lampshade. (Think thin. Excessive paint will block out light and appear as a gray area when the shade is illuminated.) Oils also blend and shade easily. The trick to working with oils in stenciling is to use a **little** paint worked into a stencil brush. Rub out excess paint onto a paper towel until you almost think you do not have enough paint to work with. Very lightly work the paint into a stencil or theorem plate opening onto the paper. I apply just a thin layer of paint, then with a clean brush, rub to soften it. Start with this very light coat of paint and slowly add more color to deepen and shade. You must keep the light areas as light as possible with this first layer. Do not rely on white paint to lighten. White paint is opaque and will block light. If oils are used very sparingly, the paper will absorb enough paint to dry almost immediately. This is a treat since oil paints are generally slow to dry.

STENCIL

"Wheat" by Stencil Ease, MultiGroup. Used with permission.

THEOREM PAINTING

Theorem painting is a process of using multiple stencils (often referred to as plates). Theorem painting is associated with painting on velvet, however one need not be restricted to velvet. The theorem samples included in this book, the little girl and little boy, are done on paper.

Theorem cutting is the same as cutting a simple stencil except there are multiple stencils (called plates). Four properly sectioned overlaying plates are required.

The patterns of the little boy and girl are numbered to correspond with the four plates used in the stencils. Each number represents a different plate. To cut the stencils for this theorem, be sure each numbered section is cut on the proper plate. When painting through the various stencils, it is important that each be properly aligned. For more on theorem painting, refer to Ruth Ann Greenhill's book, *Early American Decoration*.

THEOREM

Brushes

Small stencil brush
#4 Stain blender
#0 or #1 Round

Palette for Boy and Girl

White (W)
Burnt Sienna (BS)
Cadmium Red Light (CRL)
Yellow Ochre (YO)
Cerulean Blue (CB)
Payne's Gray (PG)
Asphaltum (Asph)
Olive Green (OG)
Black (B)

Boy and Girl

Flesh - W + BS + CRL + YO
Dress and Jeans - CB + PG + W
   (This is called Blue Mix)
Shirt and Blouse - W + Blue Mix
Hair - Asph
Eyes - Blue Mix + PG
Grass - OG

Boy

Apple - CRL
Bookcover - BU
Pages - W + YO
Boy's strap - B
Buckets - BU

Girl

Lunch pail - CRL
Shoes - PG
Chalk board - B + BU

The numerals on the design refer to the various stencil plates on which each design portion is to be traced. If you wish to simply paint the design directly, ignore the numerals.

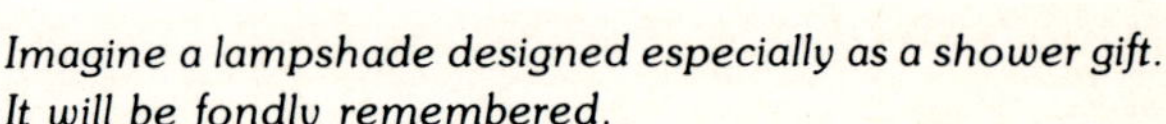

Imagine a lampshade designed especially as a shower gift.
It will be fondly remembered.

GLASS PAINTING TECHNIQUE - OIL PAINTS ON ACETATE

This technique is very beautiful on a lampshade. Any design that is suitable for pen and ink will paint well. I will not attempt to give directions because it has been so well done by other painting teachers. Sherry Nelson has graciously permitted the inclusion in this book lampshades featuring three of her designs:

"Bluejay," *Glass Giraffe, Vol. I,* page 50
"Flowers and bumblebee," *Glass Giraffe, Vol. II,* page 41
"Violets with Butterfuly," *Begin with Butterflies,* page 66

Follow directions for making the cut and pierced shade, omitting cutting, piercing, and lining. Trace the design with pen and ink directly onto the shiny side of the acetate which was cut for your shade. Use "waterproof ink for film."

Paint the design using transparent oil colors to which a tiny drop of cobalt drier has been added. Apply paint thinly to permit fast drying. Hang to dry. Note: While working with the acetate, you may want to wear a thin, cheap pair of cotton gloves to avoid fingerprinting the acetate. This is not necessary, but it certainly saves lots of cleaning up later.

After the paint has thoroughly dried, continue assembling the lampshade as per directions for the cut and pierced shade.

Lampshades open up a whole new area for those who paint. Can you think of a lovelier showcase? Paintings cannot be overlooked, particularly at night. It's like putting a spotlight on your painting without looking like a "show-off."

"Bluejay" pattern from **Glass Giraffe, Vol. I,**
©Sherry Nelson. Used with permission.

"Bluejay" pattern from **Glass Giraffe, Vol. I,**
©Sherry Nelson. Used with permission..

Color page: Two reverse glass designs by Sherri Nelson and cut and pierce shade on folk art rocking horse.

DECORATIVE FOLK ART

By using a little imagination, a few basic brush strokes, and coordinating colors, one can create some very special lamps to fit a decorating theme. The two decorative folk art lamps shown on the color pages were painted by Jackie Shaw with the young child in mind. The toy rocking horse was converted to a lamp base and decorated with an array of scrolls and simple flowers. This technique of painting is illustrated in Jackie's book, *Rock 'N Tole.* I have added a cut and pierced shade repeating the horse theme.

The other folk art lamp features a pull toy, "Sir Shelley" from Jackie's book, *Jackie's Toy Box.* The toy sits on a wooden base and may be removed for play. Any toy or other decorative accessory or collectible would work equally well as the focal point for a lamp. The shade is then coordinated to match. In this case, a border design of simple strokes was painted in acrylics around the top and bottom of the shade using the same colors as those used on the pull toy. Since the strokes are heavy and opaque, they were kept close to the edges of the shade. If a larger design is to be painted on a shade in acrylics, the paints should be thinned to permit greater transparency. Otherwise the opaque design will not reflect light when the lamp is turned on, and will appear as just a grey area.

What fun children's lampshades are. A child will love his or her very own animal or toy on a lampshade or as part of the base. Perhaps the child can even draw his or her own design for the shade.

©Marion Pond 1981

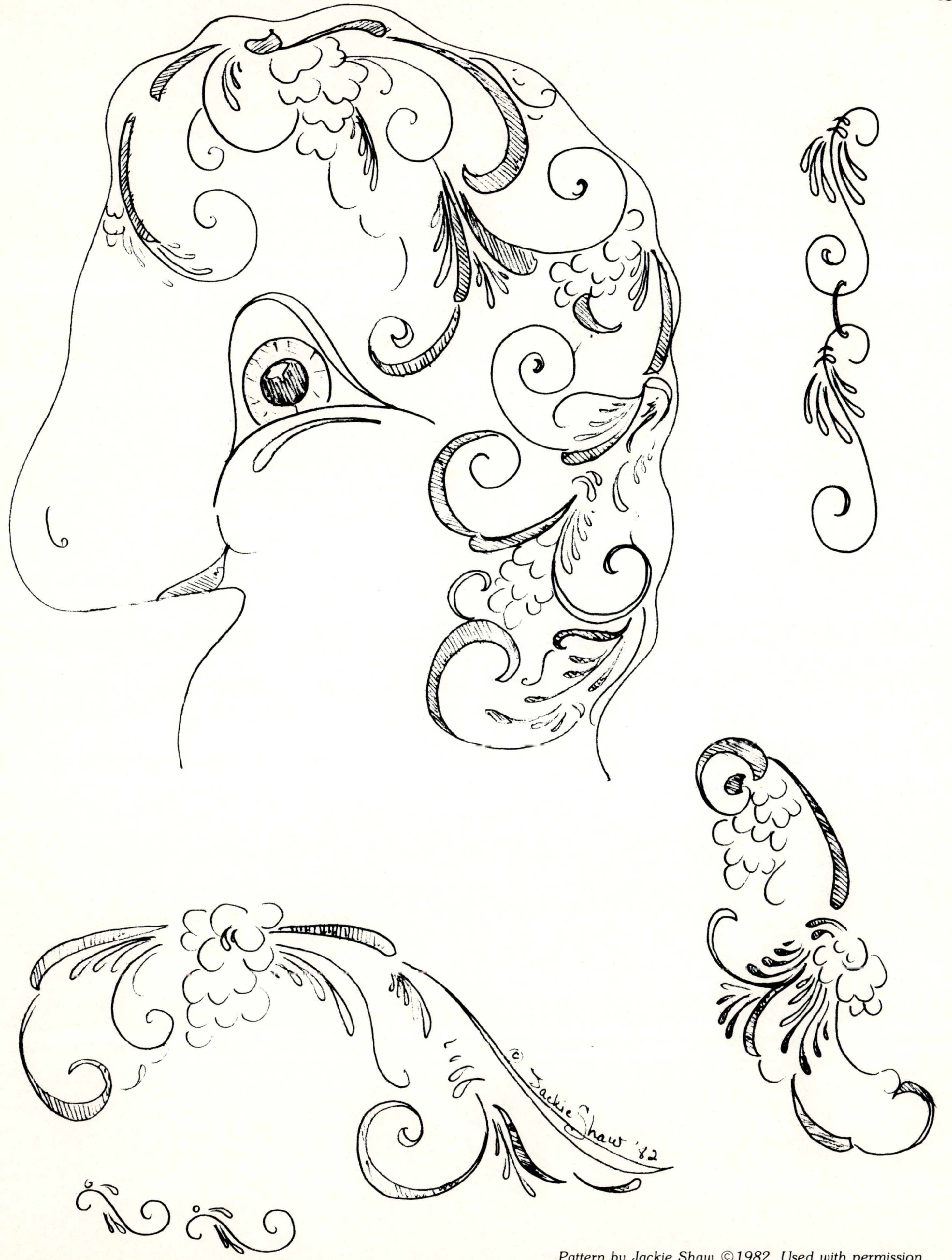

EASY WATERCOLOR METHOD

Water color is a lovely medium for paper. Many of the papers we use are water color papers so we have a perfect surface. The technique is easy, clean and fun. Water colors also have the transparency that is so desirable on a lampshade.

Even the non-painter can do a super job on the first try by following these easy directions and working one section at a time. On a cut and pierced shade, you need not paint as detailed as is necessary on other painting surfaces because the molding of the paper picks up the light and does much of the shading for you.

Follow the directions for making a cut and pierced lampshade through the piercing and cutting stage. Before molding and lining, turn the shade over to the front. (Some painters paint on the backside, but I prefer painting on the front.)

Lift a section of the design, slip a piece of scrap shade paper under this section. The scrap will catch any paint that might run over the edge. Use a #4 or #6 flat brush. The size brush you use is determined by the size of the area you are painting, small area, small brush, larger areas, larger brush. Dip the brush into clean water. Lightly touch your brush to a folded paper towel to remove excess water. Dampen the painting area, do not flood it. By dampening the area first, your color will not "grab" and you will be able gradually to add color and blend. Now dip the brush into water again, carry water in your brush and mix with a very *small* amount of paint, making a light wash. Once again touch the paper towel to remove excess. Then test the color on a scrap of paper. It is much harder to remove color than to add it, so start light and **gradually** add more color to deepen and to shade. Always touch excess water colors off on the paper towel before returning to your painting and you will be working damp, not wet. *WORK DAMP AND ADD COLOR GRADUALLY.* Work only one section at a time.

To add the finishing touches use a liner or #1 round brush to paint the detail work, being careful not to have colors extremely dark. The paint should be of ink consistency. Paint in flower centers, veins in leaves. On a straight cut, like stems and branches, paint a fine line close to the edge of the cut.

Helpful hints: Color can be removed by flooding the area with clean water and blotting with a paper towel. Keep repeating this process. The result may not always be perfect but it will be much improved. The eraser is not helpful removing watercolors. You are more apt to be pleased if your painting is delicate in color, than if it is vivid.

A dramatic color statement may be made by adding watercolor tints to the design. (See the Easy Watercolor Method on page 44.)

Brushes
#4 or #6 Flat
#0 or #1 Round

Palette for Strawberry Design

Grumbacher Red (GR)
Alizarin Crimson (AC)
Cadmium Yellow Medium (CYM)
Green Earth (GE)
Burnt Umber (BU)
Burnt Sienna (BS)

Strawberries - CYM (highlight), GR, AC (shade)
Leaves - GE, BU (shade)
Flower centers - CYM, BS
Flowers - CYM, CYM + BS (shade and vein)
Stems - GE

Palette for Dogwood

Hooker's Green (HG)
Alizarin Crimson (AC)
Cadmium Yellow Light (CYL)
White (W)

Flowers - AC (very light wash), HG (very light wash near centers, blend out), AC (shade)
Flower centers - HG, CYL + W (dab in)
Leaves - HG (wash and shade)
Branch - BU

When your lamps are suffering from the "blahs," give them a "pick-me-up" with a new shade. A bright, new change (hat, face, or hairdo) can lift anyone's spirits -even a lamp's.

TRAPUNTO

Trapunto is an old needle craft art used to create raised designs in quilting. Trapunto on a lampshade involves sculpting a shape from a designed fabric by padding or filling the design with polyester fiberfill to give it contours. Any design which can be completely cut out of a fabric can be used for Trapunto. (See the large shade with blue and beige flowers and the smaller shade with the deer). Avoid loose woven materials and designs with too many little shapes. Stitch Witchery (available in fabric stores) may be used to give body to lightweight fabrics, and to prevent edges from unraveling. Follow manufacturer's directions.

Cut an arc and cover it with a fabric that is a suitable background for the design you will be padding. Follow directions for pressure sensitive adhesive backings to provide stability for the fabric.

When the arc is cut and covered with the fabric of your choice, lay it out flat and position the cut design. Starting in the center and working out toward the edge, glue and stuff with 100% polyester fiberfill, completing one section at a time. The 100% polyester fiberfill is not dense or lumpy, and it pulls apart easily, making it light and fluffy. These features permit light to show through evenly.

Finish construction using a pressure sensitive adhesive backing. This is a material that will allow you to use almost any fabric or paper in a lampshade. It is a sticky surface covered with a removable paper covering. To use fabrics or papers - just cut a shade arc, add ½ inch to one seam. Lay this down, peel a little paper back on one end and start pressing your fabric on to this sticky surface. Peel and press fabric on, a little at a time, working to the end. Trim excess fabric from remaining edges. If using fabric, score a line on that added ½ inch line and remove this extra ½ inch of material to glue and turn over to the inside. This makes a neat, non-raveling back seam.

Follow construction directions (for cut and pierced lampshades) omitting cutting, piercing, lining and acetate. Instead of fastening seam with brads, use glue, Trim as directed.

Coordinate your drapes or upholstery with a fabric lampshade.

REFERENCES

Reverse glass painting
  Glass Giraffe, Vols. I and II
  Begin With Butterflies
    Sherry Nelson
    The Magic Brush, Inc.
    P.O. Box 868
    Anthony, TX 88021

Theorem painting
  Early American Decoration
    Ruth Ann Greenhill
    51 Platt Lane
    Milford, CT 06460

Drafting patterns
  Sculptured Lampshades
    Ruth Dorsman
    Unique Creations, Inc.
    28 Cherokee Drive
    Newark, DE 19713

Decorative Folk Art
  Rock 'N Tole
  Jackie's Toy Box
    Decorative Design Studio
    RR 3, Box 155
    Smithsburg, MD 21783

For more information regarding lampshade making and decorating contact Marion Pond at Brentwood Lampshade, South Road, Brentwood, NH 03833

SOURCES

Stencil designs and materials
  J&P Distributors
  P.O. Box 311
  Jaffrey, NH 03452

Lampshade materials
  Red Barn Distributors
  16 Scott Street
  S. Attleboro, MA 02703

Brushes
  Loew Cornell
  131 W. Ruby Avenue
  Palisades Park, NJ 07650

Glue Gizzmo and designs
  Brentwood Lampshade
  South Road
  Brentwood, NH 03833

This book has just scratched the surface of Decorative Lampshades. Once you have learned the basic construction techniques you'll be delighted as you try new ideas.

Back cover: Cut and pierce designs by the author.